DARTMOOR
A TIMELESS LANDSCAPE

by Josephine M Collingwood

DARTMOOR NATIONAL PARK - Official Visitor Guide

Published in Great Britain by:
Tavicinity Publishing
Fairways, Coryton, Okehampton, Devon EX20 4PB
email: tavicinity@dartmoor-tors.co.uk
www.dartmoor-tors.co.uk

A Cataloguing-in-Publication (CIP) record of this book is available from the British Library.

First printed in July 2018.

Typesetting and origination by Tavicinity Publishing.

978-1-9997405-2-8

Printed and bound in Devon, England by Short Run Press Limited, Exeter.

Front cover: Haytor Rocks
Back Cover: River Walkham at Grenofen

CONTENTS

Lyd Valley view over Dartmoor in the 'Golden Hour'

Higher Tor in winter snow

INTRODUCTION

Dartmoor can be described as many things: Britain's most southerly wilderness, a world-class landscape for geology and an area of extraordinary archaeology. However, for many it is a timeless landscape of unmitigated wonder.

Ask the people who live here, work here and play here why they love it, or even why they may hate it, and the answers may well be the same! The rain, mist, and bogs can repel the uninitiated just as much it might excite the Dartmoor enthusiast. Windy, rainy yomps on the moor can even make some people grin with excitement, especially those who are members of the Dartmoor Search & Rescue Teams.

This book aims to serve up the essence of Dartmoor on a platter for those who want the taster menu. There are so many excellent books that cover specific aspects of the moor for those who want more detailed information. For casual visitors and those who want an overview, this book is for you.

A word of warning; Dartmoor gets under the skin. The photographs in this book depict a vibrant National Park that is beautiful and alluring. Get to know it a bit more and you will see beyond the colours. The scents, textures, contrasts, wilderness and heritage start to lay the foundations of a passion that adheres forever to the subconscious. Dartmoor's lasting impressions are not pictorial but synaesthetic - a multitude of senses sculpt the memories of Dartmoor. You'll be back for more before you know it.

Before you head out into the living, working museum remember two things: firstly that Dartmoor can sometimes be dangerous and due care and preparation must be undertaken before exploring it, and secondly that it is a national treasure; please treat it with respect.

Black-a-Ven Brook near Cullever Steps

Great Staple Tor - a classic avenue tor with tall granite stacks

GEOLOGY AND LANDSCAPE

Formation of Dartmoor

Dartmoor is essentially a granite upland that was formed some 290 million years ago. When the planet was undergoing massive forces that created mountains and new continents, an immense volume of molten granite formed under the Devonian and Carboniferous rocks of Devon and Cornwall.

Over a few million years this magma, which was less dense than the surrounding rocks, rose up to the surface of the Earth's crust. It baked and altered the sedimentary rocks surrounding it to form the 'metamorphic aureole' and then cooled to create the granite uplands that crop up from Dartmoor down through Cornwall to beyond the Isles of Scilly.

Dartmoor's landscape has the biggest area of exposed granite in the South West and, like all landscapes, it has been defined by the rock beneath it. Granite determines the soil that forms on the surface, which in turn determines the type of vegetation that grows upon it. The rock's structure also affects how water flows off it, or not - as seen in blanket bogs. Add in the nature of the rock intrusion which created areas of extraordinary mineral wealth and you have a unique and fascinating landscape.

As the granite cooled it formed joints and was subjected to millions of years of chemical erosion. The tropical forests above the land meant that rotting vegetation formed acid waters that percolated into the granite from above. This water gradually decomposed some of the granite. So even though the top of the granite was underneath the surface, much of its structure was being created beneath.

Watern Tor thurlestone formation

7

Winter view from Hare Tor towards Fur Tor.

Dartmoor returns to Ice Ages tundra, just for a little while.

Ice Age Erosion

Weathered joints on Honeybag Tor

Growan surrounding 'buried tor' at Two Bridges

Although the granite was intruded some 290 million years ago, the granite we see today as hilltop tors was not exposed until relatively recently: around 45,000 years ago. However, it had already been weathered underground by extensive chemical alteration and later by the Ice Ages (between about 600,000 to 10,000 years ago). Where the acidic ground water of a warm climate left off, freeze-thaw action began.

Freeze-thaw action is when rain water in cracks and indents freezes and expands, forcing the crack wider; perhaps even splitting the rock in two. When thawed, more water is allowed in and process repeats. Dartmoor's post Ice Age landscape is regarded as a world-class example.

Even though the granite was still buried, it came closer to the surface as the overlying material was eroded. A mass of broken down granite material called 'growan' formed around the granite, which was loose and easily removed.

At **Two Bridges**, in the middle of Dartmoor, there is a car park (for the path to **Wistman's Wood**) which has a 'buried tor' as a backdrop. It illustrates how a familiar-looking granite outcrop can be already weathered and shaped before its overburden of growan is removed.

The Ice Ages made relatively short work of removing the growan layers and exposing the tors to the full force of surface weathering and erosion. Granite outcrops have literally been prised apart and shattered by freeze-thaw, littering the slopes with broken rocks of all sizes. These boulders are collectively called 'clitter' and can be a serious challenge for walkers' ankle welfare.

Freeze-thaw splits the granite at Shelstone Tor

Mineral Wealth

When the huge mass of granite magma cooled down, it solidified into hard rock. At the same time it released hydrothermal fluids laden with chemical elements. These were released under enormous pressure and high temperatures, forcing their way through rocks and joints creating mineral veins when they solidified.

When these hydrothermal solutions cooled down, the minerals crystallised, but at different temperatures. This created a zoning of minerals, with tin and tungsten found closest to the granite heat source. Copper, lead and iron formed the furthest away, having the lowest crystallisation temperature.

This banding of minerals is found all around Dartmoor at the metamorphic aureole and also at 'emanative centres' of localised hydrothermal activity.

Thus Dartmoor's granite has given the area significant metallurgic wealth: with mining for tin, copper, lead, silver, haematite (iron) and tungsten forming an important part of its history. The remnants of mining activities can be found all over Dartmoor, both ancient and modern in age.

It is not metallurgic mining that is dominant today, however. The weathering of granite from hot acidic hydrothermal fluids created large areas of decomposed granite which formed kaolin or 'china clay'.

This is a valuable commodity and has been mined on Dartmoor for hundreds of years. The china clay works on the south of Dartmoor around **Lee Moor** are vast and constitute a major industry for contemporary Dartmoor.

Mineral veins in altered granite

Remains of Vitifer Tin Mine

Lee Moor China Clay Works

Roos Tor and Great Mis Tor behind.

A steely cold day strips away the colour to reveal the textures of the rocky landscape.

13

The Dartmoor Landscape

As the largest and highest upland area in Southern Britain, Dartmoor has poor acid soils, high rainfall and strong winds. These elements preclude intensive farming, allowing a more natural environment to survive, revealing a unique and beguiling landscape that evokes long-lasting obsession and loyalty, in spite of the rain.

The landscape changes from the high plateaus of moorland heath and bog to the deep valleys of post glacial rivers which carved through the rock at an accelerated rate.

In terms of geology, Dartmoor is the largest area of unglaciated upland in England and as such is of great importance in geological and geophysical study.

Uplands

The upland area of Dartmoor can be characterised by two main plateau areas in the north and south, with a tilt over the whole region from north west to south east. The highest areas of the granite upland are thus on the north of Dartmoor, with **High Willhays** reaching an altitude at 621 metres - the highest point in Southern England. High Dartmoor is wild, bleak and devoid of trees.

The impermeable bedrock of granite has led to vast areas of poorly drained bogs and the build up of peat over the last few thousand years. In some places the peat is several metres deep, and in the past formed the main fuel source for both local people and the mining industry. Even in high summer, the bogs stay wet; it is no wonder that 45% of the South West's drinking water is sourced from Dartmoor.

High Moorland on North Dartmoor

High Willhays - highest point in Southern England

Peat hags on High Dartmoor

Mosses cling to the boulders in the River Erme

Rivers

Many of Devon's rivers have their source on the high plateaus of Dartmoor. On the northern plateau are the heads of the Dart, Tavy and Walkham rivers which flow south, with the Rivers Taw, West Okement and East Okement draining off north. The southern plateau is drained by the Plym, Meavy, Erme, Yealm and Avon. The River Bovey and Teign drain the east of the moor. Rivers are an integral part of Dartmoor's landscape and character, with swift flowing water sliding around big rounded boulders in the green shade of oaks, hazel and beech trees.

Broadleaf woodland in river valley

River Tavy cascading down Tavy Cleave on Western Dartmoor

Clam Bridge over the Colly Brook near Peter Tavy

During thawing from the Ice Ages, the rivers were in more or less a constant state of deluge. They moved vast amounts of boulders, rocks and minerals down the valleys, dropping the material wherever they slowed down.

Dartmoor's typical river valley thus sees large boulders amid a mass of smaller ones, rounded by the constant abrasive action of water and rock. The river water skirts between these large boulders, giving little hint of previous torrents. Mosses and lichens have taken hold of exposed boulder surfaces.

Woodland

Where Dartmoor is incised by rivers, there is shelter and a different landscape. On the high moor, there are ancient woodlands of oaks whose roots cling to boulders on the river banks. These high oak groves are particularly special and contain many rare species of fern and lichen - a testament to the clean, unpolluted air on the moor.

Lower down, where the rock changes, the rivers have carved much deeper valleys and gorges, with steep sides cloaked in deciduous trees.

Broadleaf woodland at Burrator

Farmland

At the edges of Dartmoor and in the lower reaches of the rivers, the landscape becomes undulating and more fertile as soils are richer and deeper. Here, farms dominate the landscape, enclosing fields for pasture. The landscape changes from browns to greens.

Deciduous woodland by the River Teign

Farmland in the central basin of Dartmoor, near Bellever

Bronze Age stone row and cairn circle near Down Tor

HERITAGE

The fact that we can see so much archaeology today is because of climate change. Around 1000 years ago the climate changed and it became colder and wetter. This meant that farming cereals became increasingly difficult as they would not ripen and dry (drying barns found at a medieval village near **Hound Tor** show our forebears' plight in trying to continue farming cereals). Within a few hundred years, farming moved off the moor and to the margins. The high moorland was left for summer grazing only and has remained so ever since. The onslaught of modern civilisation and its voracious need for land and resource has passed the high Dartmoor lands by, as they are simply unsuitable for anything other than marginal animal grazing.

The consequence of this is a landscape still encrusted by the archaeological remains of our ancestors. To walk over Dartmoor is to walk through time.

Mesolithic Period (8000BC to 4000BC)

After the ice sheets retreated north and tundra conditions ended around 10,000 years ago, woodlands started to flourish, providing a perfect habitat for grazing animals.

At this time, Dartmoor was covered by vast oak, hazel and elm woodlands, with patches of open heath around the highest tors. Around 8,000 years ago, settlers started to change the landscape by clearing the edges of the woodland to create better land for foraging animals like deer; hunting them became easier that way. Areas of flat high ground developed peat where decomposing vegetation trapped in poorly drained areas

Granite tramway near Haytor

King's Barrow on Hameldown

amassed. As the tree line receded down the valley sides, areas of peat bog expanded and the woodlands were less able to re-establish in some areas. The climate got better over the generations and the early settlers changed from a nomadic lifestyle of hunter gathering to that of herders and farmers. With good land and predictable resources, it made sense to stay and settle.

Neolithic Period (4000BC and 2500BC)

In Neolithic times, both animals and crops were domesticated and deliberate food planting was introduced. Study of pollen has indicated that some woodland was cleared and replaced by cultivated herbs and grasses.

Spinster's Rock burial chamber

Dartmoor's earliest structures date back to this period. Stone burial chamber tombs and earth mounds called barrows or dolmens still stand and can be visited. **Spinster's Rock** is the best example, although it has been rebuilt. It is easily accessible, situated close to the lane between **Drewsteignton** and **Shilstone**, at the north east corner of the National Park. Other probable Neolithic structures are low walls that encircle tors. There are two such sites at **Dewerstone** and **White Tor** that may have been 'territorial centres'.

Bronze Age (2000BC to 600BC)

Scorhill Stone Circle

Settlers adapted and created settlements on the lower slopes of the moorland. The Bronze Age represents a hiatus of activity on Dartmoor. Hundreds of settlements are evidenced all over the area along with ceremonial sites, ritual burial locations and a highly sophisticated system of agricultural divisions in the form of reaves. Dartmoor's Bronze Age archaeology is renowned worldwide and allows visitors to discover whole Bronze Age landscapes; illustrating how our ancestors lived, worked and died over 3000 years ago.

Merrivale Double Stone Row

Monuments
Upright stones arranged in circles and rows are thought to be associated with burials, whereas large stone circles may have been for ritualistic ceremonies. In truth, nobody knows precisely, but their importance at the time of construction as well as today cannot be overstated. Whatever their original purpose, they retain their supernal ambience.

There are around 75 stone rows and 18 stone circles found in Dartmoor National Park, as well as over 1500 burial cairns, which constitutes the largest concentration in all of Britain.

Menhir at Drizzlecombe

Burial Cists
Within some cairn circles, and sometimes alone, there are over 200 burial chambers scattered all over the moor. They are in the form of granite 'boxes' with a larger granite slab placed on top. Known as cists (pronounced "kists"), they contained human remains or more commonly, cremations. In 2011, a newly discovered cist on **Whitehorse Hill** was excavated. Inside was an exceptional collection of early Bronze Age grave goods, including organic material.

The excavation revealed cremated remains wrapped in an animal pelt (almost certainly a native brown bear). Inside the pelt was a woven basket containing 200 beads, some wooden studs, a wristband of woven cow hair and tin, and a flint tool. The beads were a mixture of amber, tin, shale and clay.

Whitehorse Hill burial cist

Grimspound Bronze Age settlement

Easily explored by walking up from the lane near Hameldown, this spectacular Bronze Age settlement contains 24 hut circle remains. It illustrates how a village of homes and animal pens was protected by a substantial circular 'pound' or wall.

Hut circle on Shapley Common

Settlements

The people who lived and farmed on the moor built their homes and livestock shelters out of the materials at hand. Circular granite huts with wood and thatch roofs were constructed all over the moor. Today there are around 5000 hut circles identified on Dartmoor; their round granite walls, built so well, clearly remain. The hut circles had doors, porches and room divisions; our ancestors lived in relative comfort. Many large settlements made use of good drainage and water supplies. One of the best preserved is at **Grimspound** which is well worth a visit.

Towards the end of the Bronze Age, the climate was deteriorating; rainfall increased and temperatures cooled making farming more difficult. The result was a gradual abandonment of the high moorland settlements; people and farming moved to the valleys and edges of the moor, where more favourable conditions allowed them to continue farming.

Hut circle at Grimspound settlement

Iron Age (600BC to 43AD)

There is not as much evidence of human settlements for this period, when iron became more prevalent in the manufacture of tools and weapons. This is probably because it has been overlain by subsequent settlement and changed land use. What survives is a series of hillforts which indicates a different approach to settlement. A good example is **Brentor** on western Dartmoor; on the slopes below the church are the earthwork remains of an Iron Age hillfort.

Hillforts were usually located on high ground above wooded valleys with substantial defences of ramparts and ditches. Life at this time must have been more volatile.

Brentor - Iron Age hillfort site

Roman Britain and Dark Ages (43AD to 700AD)

The enormous changes to Britain under Roman rule seem to have had little effect on Dartmoor judging by the lack of evidence from this period. Celtic culture prevailed until the Saxons conquered Devon in 805AD.

Saxon Stone at Sourton

Saxon and Medieval Period (700AD to 1540AD)

The population of Dartmoor during the Saxon period was evidently sparse; some Saxon memorial stones have been found on the periphery. One such stone has been re-erected at **Sourton**. An exception to this is **Lydford**; one of the Devon burhs (or 'boroughs') designated by Alfred the Great. The original Saxon street plan and earthwork defences still survive and can be explored today.

In 1240, Dartmoor's status of "Royal Forest" was changed to that of a "Chase" by King Henry III who gifted it to his brother Richard, Earl of Cornwall. The land was then reclaimed by Edward III in 1337 who gifted it to his son Edward the Black Prince, Duke of Cornwall. A charter ruled that the eldest son and heir to the throne would have the title of Duke of Cornwall. From then until now, much of Dartmoor remains the property of the Duchy of Cornwall.

11th century earthworks of Lydford

In 1240 a 'Perambulation' to delineate the Forest boundary was undertaken; markers and features were used to define royal lands. Settlements within the Forest boundary started to appear, taking advantage of a period of warmer climate. These medieval settlements and tenant farms became known as 'Ancient Tenements'. Special boundary walls called 'cornditches' were built where a ditch was faced with a tall

Medieval cornditch boundary wall

Clapper bridge at Postbridge

Dartmoor's most popular and visited clapper bridge; it is very close to the road and probably dates back to around 1300AD.

Teign-e-Ver clapper bridge

Remains of medieval tin streaming

Mortar stone from tin stamping mill

stone wall with a build up of material behind it. This prevented royal deer from entering the tenement farms whilst allowing any that did an easy way back.

The farmsteads and hamlets were linked by narrow lanes and tracks with humpback granite bridges and clapper bridges where they crossed rivers and streams. On the fringes of the moor, larger towns grew in size, benefiting from the wealth generated by wool and tin.

Clapper Bridges

These medieval bridges are simple in design but enchanting to explore. Walk over one and feel 700 years slip away. Built from large slabs of granite, they allowed people and pack-horses to cross streams and rivers safely. Many are small spans across streams. Larger ones, like those at **Postbridge** and **Dartmeet**, are multi-span bridges set on strong tall pillars of stone, shaped to deflect floodwaters. Dartmoor's clapper bridges literally paved the way for transporting goods, allowing medieval industry to thrive.

Medieval Industry

Dartmoor's mineral wealth meant that tin was almost certainly mined from the Bronze Age, when is would have been alloyed with copper to form bronze tools and weapons. Pewter (using higher concentrations of tin) became commonplace from around 600AD. However, the earliest hard evidence of tin mining dates back to the 12th century. It is probable that older tin workings would have been obliterated by later excavations.

The medieval tinners worked the streams and rivers over the whole moor extracting tin ore, called cassiterite, left in the fluvial deposits. They dug out the river banks, sluiced the material and processed the ore in tin stamping mills and smelting houses before carting tin ingots off the moor to be weighed and coined at one of the four Stannary Towns. You can explore these old building ruins and find ingot mould stones, water wheel pits and mortar stones. Mortar stones are slabs of rock where tin ore was crushed by wooden stamp heads powered by a water wheel. The stamp heads pounded the ore into gravel ready to smelt; like a great pestle and mortar. Countless blows created rounded bowls in the slab; when it got too deep, the slab was moved and a new bowl would start to form.

Mould stone for smelted tin ingots

As well as tin, peat was dug from the vast reserves on the high moor in order to fuel the smelting furnaces on the moor as well as providing domestic fuel.

Medieval Farming

With Dartmoor turning into a working landscape and its population increasing, more home-grown food was needed to feed the people. It is thought that the Normans re-introduced rabbits to Britain, which provided both food and fur. Rabbits were bred in warrens, situated well away from other farms. There were over 20 medieval warrens on Dartmoor. Rabbits were bred in constructed cigar-shaped pillow mounds orientated downhill for drainage. Strategically placed vermin traps were constructed from stone and slate to control the population of stoats and weasels. The traps are shaped like a large 'X' and are designed to funnel the vermin into a trap in the middle.

Pillow mound near Little Trowlesworthy Tor

Medieval agriculture has left its mark on the land too; early methods of field cultivation shaped the topography so that we can still see the remains of field systems today.

Vermin trap at Trowlesworthy Warren

Strip lynchets at Challacombe

Medieval farming techniques can be seen on the slopes above Challacombe Medieval Village. Ploughs were driven along the contour of the hill, creating a strip of usable land where the soil built up before a bank defining the lower strip. Over time, these terraces became more pronounced. The fact that Challacombe's strips were still defined in the 18th century and that they have not been over-ploughed means the medieval archaeology has survived.

Dartmoor longhouse - Higher Uppacott

Higher Uppacott lane and gate

Dartmoor Longhouse

The Dartmoor longhouse is a typical medieval farmstead building, some of which are still occupied today, albeit as a highly modernised version. The original stone rectangular building was crossed by a central passage, with the upper side of the passage providing the living area for the farmer and his family. The lower side was the shippon where the animals were kept. One room and roof meant that both animals and people could share the warmth of a central hearth fire. Smoke was allowed to drift up and through the thatch.

Higher Uppacott shippon

The shippon had a drain running down the centre, with space for tethered animals each side.

Higher Uppacott

Dartmoor National Park owns the Grade I listed medieval farmhouse of Higher Uppacott, near **Poundsgate**. It is a classic Dartmoor longhouse which dates back to the 14th century and retains the original animal shippon. Large granite cobbles form a central drain, with upright kerbs near the

Floor cobbles of Higher Uppacott shippon

Open thatched roof of Higher Uppacott shippon

Back of Higher Uppacott

outer walls drilled for tethering posts. Over the centuries, the farmhouse was subdivided by walls and had many 'modern' additions - a large fireplace and chimney stack in the 16th century and a first floor and new roof in the 17th century.

This extraordinary longhouse is a portal back through time on Dartmoor and is an absolutely fascinating place for anyone with even the slightest interest in history.

Guided visits are available through the National Park Authority.

Leats

Medieval engineers became highly skilled at directing the course of waterways for their own purpose. Water wheels in mills relied on a constant head of water to work, as did tin miners who used the flowing water to sluice the stone and earth material to extract tin ore. Homesteads and settlements also needed a constant supply of clean water.

Devonport Leat and aqueduct over River Meavy

Techniques for building these water channels, known locally as 'leats', improved over the years so that water could be efficiently transported over moorland for many miles, following the contours of the hills. Accurate surveying was essential to ensure a constant and steady flow of water. When leats had to cross other water courses, small aqueducts were built.

In the late 1500s, Plymouth needed a reliable clean water supply. An Act of Parliament in 1585 gave permission for the town to construct a leat from Dartmoor to Plymouth. This project was overseen by Sir Francis Drake in 1591. The channel for '**Drake's Leat**' was dug from what is now under Burrator Reservoir, all the way into Plymouth: a distance of 18.5 miles (29 km), with a drop in height of only 10 metres.

'Sheep leap' over Devonport Leat

As Plymouth Dock (now called Devonport, a separate town from Plymouth at the time) expanded over the centuries, more water was needed. Two hundred years after Drake's Leat, another was built that brought water from three of Dartmoor's rivers over a distance of 27 miles (43 km) into Devonport.

The '**Devonport Leat**' took 7 years to build and still flows, although it now finishes near Burrator reservoir. Many leats are still in use today and some Dartmoor communities are still supplied by 'Pot Water Leats', built to supply drinking water.

Wheal Jewell Mine Leat near Tavy Cleave

Newtake wall near Shapley Tor

Ruins at Foggintor Quarry

Modern Era

'Improvers'

There was a period of time, towards the end of the 18th century, when great effort was spent in trying to 'improve' Dartmoor's agriculture. It was during the new era of science, innovation and industrialisation. Tracks across the moor became turnpiked; officially administered and maintained. Wealthy landowners built new farms, applied fertilisers and new farming techniques to raise the yield of the land.

Through licences granted by the Duchy, they also enclosed large tracts of open moorland for more intensive agricultural use. These were 'Newtakes', bounded by hastily built stone walls which still remain.

The most famous 'Improver' was Sir Thomas Tyrwhitt who built his own Tor Royal Estate at **Princetown** in 1785. He also built much of Princetown itself, Dartmoor Prison and new farms at Bachelor's Hall, Peat Cot and Swincombe using granite from Foggintor quarry. He built a horse-drawn granite tramway linking the quarry to the Plymouth and Dartmoor Railway which opened in 1823 to transport commodities to and from the moor.

Foggintor is a fascinating place to visit; easily accessed along the track past **Yellowmead Farm**, visitors can explore the quarry itself which has taken on a beauty of its own, as well as the ruins of the quarry buildings and tramway. Imagine it in the mid 1800s when there were 300 men working there and some 30 families living there.

Ultimately, the 'Improvers' were defeated by the immutable characteristics of Dartmoor's climate and soils. Over-optimism, a touch of arrogance and money could not tame Dartmoor.

Granite tramway at Foggintor Quarry

Dartmoor Prison at Princetown

Dartmoor Prison

Constructed between 1806 and 1809, Dartmoor Prison was built to house more than 5000 Napoleonic prisoners of war. These were supplemented in 1813 by American prisoners of war from the 'Forgotten' War of 1812 when Britain was in conflict with the United States. After the French were repatriated, the prison held over 6000 American prisoners until 1815. The prison was empty until 1850 when it became a penal prison to alleviate the increasingly unviable practice of sending convicts to British Colonies overseas.

Entrance to Dartmoor Prison

Wheal Betsy silver and lead mine engine house

Haytor Quarry - tranquillity after industry

Victorians

With good infrastructure already established on Dartmoor in the form of turnpiked roads across the moor and tramways that were able to transport quarried stone, the Victorians lost little time capitalising on the region's resources. The ambitious, wealthy and entrepreneurial Victorians extended the railways, built towns for the growing population and reservoirs for water storage. The focus of the capitalists was in mining and quarrying. Existing mines were dug deeper using new technologies; quarries were enlarged and multiplied.

Gun Powder Mills ruins near Postbridge

Gunpowder required for mining and quarrying was produced near Postbridge at **Powder Mills**, where sulphur, saltpetre and charcoal were carefully ground together in widely spaced mill buildings so that any explosion could not ignite the whole site.

Some optimistic Victorians also established more risky schemes to make money, including an ice factory on the slopes of **Sourton Tors**, a glass factory near **Okehampton**, naphtha distilleries and even a starch factory near **Stannon Tor** where potatoes were grown to produce starch.

Ice factory on slopes of Sourton Tors

Site of starch factory near Stannon Tor

600 yard range marker near Hart Tor

Trenches dug for training during Boer Wars

Many business owners and workers made money during this period of expansion, but more often than not Dartmoor proved itself to be both underestimated and uncompromising. Time after time, business failed after a short period of frantic activity.

However, an important change in the perception of Dartmoor happened at this time. The Romantic Period peaked between 1800 and 1850 when writers, poets and artists expressed emotions inspired by nature. Dartmoor quickly changed from "Squalida Montana" a description from 1586 that needs no translation, to "a scene of unsurpassed loveliness" in 1842 from Samual Rowe. Dartmoor became an attractive location to visit.

Military

Military heritage on Dartmoor goes back to the need for armed guards at Dartmoor Prison. The soldiers used a rifle range near **Hart Tor** to practice their musketry. The range markers can still be seen. It was around 1850 when the Military started to use the moor for more intensive training; using the wilderness to prepare soldiers for the Crimean, Zulu and 2nd Afghan Wars from 1854 to 1880. In 1875 a permanent training area for live artillery firing was licensed, allowing troops to train for the Boer Wars; their trenches can be seen near the road from **Okehampton Army Camp**.

Target railways were built to enable training with moving targets; hidden cables and ropes pulled small trams on rails. Near to **Rowtor** there is a wonderful example of a target hut, rail system and trenches for the cables.

During the Second World War, American troops trained on Dartmoor in preparation for the Normandy landings.

Target railway shed and tramlines rails near Rowtor

Widgery's Cross on Brat Tor

William Widgery, an artist famous for his Dartmoor Landscapes paid for the construction of a granite cross on top of Brat Tor to commemorate Queen Victoria's Golden Jubilee in 1887.

43

Purple Moor Grass lining the Cowsic Valley

HABITATS AND WILDLIFE

The wide sweeping expanse of Dartmoor has many vital habitats for both plants and animals. These have been carefully studied to enhance our understanding of Dartmoor's ecosystems and how best to conserve them.

High Moorland

The high moorland is bristling with Western gorse, heather, bristle bent grass and purple moor grass. It is of international importance due to the rarity of the flora outside of the UK.

The wild bilberry grows amongst the hardy shrubs where it can avoid the attention of grazing animals keen to enjoy a juicy new shoot. Locally called 'whortleberries' or 'urts', moorlanders would gather the ripe blue-purple berries in summer to make traditional jam.

On the ground, the common lizard and adders weave amid the grasses. In the air above the heather and grass fly ravens, meadow pipits, stonechats and skylarks. In the UK, skylark numbers have more than halved in the last few decades, but on Dartmoor their numbers remain strong and their delightful songs fill the air in spring and summer.

Bracken stalks provide the rare brown fritillary butterfly with a perfect home and on the high heath, the red grouse can be spotted on occasion; resplendent with its scarlet cap and fox-red neck. Dartmoor's high moorland is also crucial for the ring ouzel; a type of black thrush with a white neck ring. Ring ouzels are in sharp decline and are closely monitored in their preferred areas of the moor.

Juniper Hair Cap Moss

45

Mires & Bogs

Dartmoor's uplands have very high rainfall (up to 2 metres per year) falling on an impervious granite bedrock and predominance of sphagnum moss. This combination leads to an accumulation of decaying plant matter that never fully decomposes; it builds up on waterlogged ground forming peat which is several metres thick in places.

On the gentle upland slopes above 400m in altitude the peat has built up to form a thick blanket of bog. There are two main areas of blanket bog on Dartmoor; the area surrounding **Cranmere Pool** in the north and the areas around **Naker's Hill** to the south. In all, there are some 8500 hectares of blanket bog on Dartmoor.

Valley mires are peat bog areas that occur below 300m and form in the shallow basins of river heads and line the river valleys as they flow away from the central moor. Blanket bogs and valley mires are hugely important habitats for rare plants and animals, but are being increasingly recognised as vitally important areas of storage for both carbon and rain water.

The dominant plant of peat bog areas is sphagnum moss. There are twelve known species on Dartmoor and they vary in colour from bright green to deep red. The plant has uses beyond that of storing water; its absorbing and cleansing properties were utilised during the WW1 when people would gather the moss to be used as wound dressings of the soldiers returning from the front.

The bog asphodel is a particularly distinctive bog plant that grows in the waterlogged ground, straight and strong, changing colour as the seasons pass.

Upland bog near Yar Tor

Sphagnum moss

Bog Asphodel

Hidden closer to the ground surface is the round-leaved sundew; our very own carnivorous plant.

The little tufts of what appears to be cotton wool balls on stalks wriggling in the wind are in fact hare's tail cotton grasses. In the lower valley mires, the bog species are supplemented by more sedges, marsh St John's wort and bog pimpernel. Frogs abound as do dragonflies and the snipe; the bogs also support rare plants such as bog orchids, as well as rare fauna such as lapwings and curlews.

Sundew carnivorous plant

Cotton grasses in moorland mires

Rhôs pasture at Challacombe Farm

Here the habitat has been conserved and thrives with abundant wildlife and wetland plants.

49

Rhôs Pasture

A special mention is required for this specific habitat that forms the transition of valley mire to lowland valley. It is an enclosed area of purple moor grass and rushes that is home to abundant and colourful wildlife. Here the meadow thistle grows alongside devil's-bit scabious, heath spotted orchid, bird's foot trefoil and marsh violet.

A particularly vibrant area of rhôs pasture can be found at **Challacombe**, near the remains of a medieval hamlet. The gently sloping valley bottom is lush with marsh plants that like their feet wet, such as marsh marigold, cuckoo flower and soft rushes.

The highly protected marsh fritillary butterfly has colonies in Dartmoor's rhôs pasture, representing about 20% of England's population. They fly among the more common marbled white and pearl-bordered fritillary butterflies and the southern damselfly - Britain's rarest damselfly.

Grass Moor

Grass moor is characterised by drier moorland areas dominated by grasses such as bristle bent, common bent, sheep's fescue and mat grasses. Gorse and heather varieties grow easily through the grasses, with bracken invading the drier slopes. Grass moorland is a product of continued heavy grazing in the past.

This is the preferred habitat for Dartmoor's larger animal inhabitants; cattle, ponies and sheep. It is also the hunting ground for predators, such as foxes and buzzards.

Bog Hoverfly on marsh marigold

Cuckoo flower in wetland

Grass moor

Bell heather in the grass moor

Woodland

Plantation Woodland
A relatively new habitat, large tracts of Dartmoor were planted with conifers after the First World War to replace timber stocks. Large plantations were established around **Fernworthy**, **Bellever**, **Soussons Down** and **Burrator**, managed by the Forestry Commission. These areas form a separate habitat for birds not commonly found on Dartmoor such as the crossbill and nightjar.

Larch plantation near Burrator

Wistman's Wood ancient oak woodland - pedunculate oak

Black-a-Tor Copse in West Okement valley

Upland Oak Woodlands

In sheltered valleys up on the high moor above 250m altitude there are the remnants of ancient oak woodlands, which have survived since the Bronze Age when much of Dartmoor's natural forest was cleared. There are three such ancient oak woodlands: **Black-a-Tor-Copse**, **Wistman's Wood** and **Piles Copse**. All three copses have almost identical situations; they are all made up of pedunculate oaks on west-facing valley sides amid dense clitter. These woods have survived both humans and climate change and are almost magical places where the roots of the stunted gnarly oaks twist among moss-covered granite boulders. The branches of the trees are covered in ferns, lichens and mosses; some of which are very rare and indicate clean, unpolluted air. It is a cornucopia of epiphytic life in every shade of green.

Wistman's Wood is easily accessible along a path from the car park near **Two Bridges** in central Dartmoor.

Wild daffodils at Dunsford Wood

Broadleaf Valley Woodlands

Where rivers have cut deep valleys, rich deciduous woodlands have flourished. They are dominated by oak, birch and rowan, with holly and hazel growing beneath their canopies.

Mosses, ferns and lichens grow profusely, with the addition of dog-violets, wild daffodils and wood anemones that appear on the woodland floor in spring. The wild daffodils at **Dunsford Woods** are particularly delightful, creating a yellow carpet of joy amid the leafless branches. Later in the year, bluebells form royal carpets through the woods, with swathes of wild garlic producing masses of white flowers. The scents are spectacular.

A hugely important inhabitant of broadleaf valley woodlands is the blue ground beetle (carabus intricatus). This extraordinary insect is Britain's largest ground beetle at up to 38mm long; it was thought to be extinct in Britain until 1994 when it was discovered on Dartmoor.

It is currently known at only a few sites, where it lives a nocturnal life, pursuing slugs up the bases of moss-covered trees. Its body is exquisitely detailed and edged with an electric blue that seems unreal.

The blue ground beetle

Bluebells at Emsworthy Farm near Haytor

Although unshaded from woodland, Emsworthy Farm and mire provide one of the best displays of bluebells on Dartmoor. It is a farm that was abandoned in the 1870s and is now maintained by the Devon Wildlife Trust. Each year, bluebells carpet the fields surrounding the ruined farm buildings. It is a haven for wildlife and when you see the bluebells be sure to listen for the cuckoo too.

Rivers

Dartmoor's beautiful rivers are fed by the upland mires and bogs which give a constant head of water. Characteristically they are fast moving with well oxygenated, unpolluted water. On the rocks along the rivers and all over the river banks, the humid habitat allow mosses, liverworts and ferns to grow. Although the water is clean, it is acidic which means the water habitats support only a specialised range of plants and animals.

Insects play a major role in the food chain of river life, supporting fish such as trout and salmon. The Brown Trout swims up and down Dartmoor's streams, leats and rivers most of its life, occasionally navigating to the sea before returning to spawn. The Atlantic Salmon, like the trout, spends its early life in the waterways before migrating to the sea. They return in late autumn to spawn, using the swollen river water to leap over weirs and obstacles.

Otters have made a good return to strength on Dartmoor where they have a national stronghold.

East Dart River near Postbridge

Farmland

The enclosed farmland of Dartmoor represents low agricultural intensity due to the nature of the soil. This allows for greater biodiversity. Large open fields, wet valleys and small woods bounded by stone walls and hedges make for an integrated habitat where wildlife is abundant. Hay meadows in particular provide a haven for wild flowers and insects.

Hay meadow near Postbridge

Between the fields there are the ancient hedgebanks so typical for Devon, where whole ecosystems can exist.

Dunnabridge farmland, central Dartmoor

Tors, Caves and Mines

Dartmoor's tors provide a perfect habitat for species that thrive on exposed sites such as lichens. There are as many as 60 different species of lichens on Dartmoor, some of which are more typical of tundra conditions in the Arctic. Caves, mine adits and dark, damp places provide a stable environment and another definitive habitat. Bats, insects, plants, water creatures and mosses all share the weak light and are sheltered from extreme conditions.

Mine entrance near River Tavy

River Teign at Fingle Bridge

Flies swarm over the water, providing ready meals for both birds and fish.

FOLKLORE AND CUSTOMS

Where to begin? Dartmoor is positively awash with tales of supernatural beings, apparitions and weird goings-on. There are many books that have been written documenting these tales, one of the best of which is Ruth St. Leger-Gordon's "*The Witchcraft and Folklore of Dartmoor*". She documents and explains the tales with rigour and a sense of rationality and scepticism, laced with a dry humour.

Let us, for this quick journey into Dartmoor's less tangible aspects, look at its folklore. As "the traditional beliefs, customs and stories of a community, passed through the generations by word of mouth" folklore is, by definition, a product of human nature. When a story is not written down but passed on in spoken word only, it tends to get embellished for a particular audience, which then passes on its own embellishments.

Lack of scientific knowledge and rationale creates a world where there is real magic and wonder, so when something cannot be explained in simple terms, we tend to make something up that can be understood.

Many stories are found all over the country, with variations and differing leading characters. There are a few, however, that are distinctly Dartmoor. And so, it is with a hefty punch of salt that I relay to you just some of Dartmoor's tales.

Childe the Hunter

Nothing like a bit of gore to start. There was a rich young landowner from Plymstock who loved to hunt alone on the moors. He was known as Childe and is thought to date back

Wisht Hound on Dartmoor

Childe's Tombe overlooking Fox Tor Mire

Childe's Tombe

to the reign of Edward III in the 1300s. The name 'Childe' is a Saxon word for youth of noble birth. In any case, he is believed to be a real person who was out on Dartmoor hunting alone in winter when a fierce snow storm swept around him. With his view obscured and his tracks disappearing rapidly he decided to wait out the storm. After a while he realised that the storm was not abating and he would freeze to death if he stayed as he was. He had a decision to make. His grim solution was to slay his own trusted horse, disembowel him and crawl inside his body for warmth.

Unfortunately, even this extreme action did not stop him from dying a cold and solitary death. His body was found entombed in his horse's frozen carcass some days later. The place was marked as "Childe's Tombe" and can be found near **Fox Tor**, south east of **Princetown**, near the infamous **Fox Tor Mire**. Go there and you will find a cross standing on a set of three octagonal steps. It is quite an impressive monument, although it has been restored several times. The site is actually an ancient burial cist from Bronze Age times (around 4000 years ago). No doubt, there was a religious need to Christianise the original site with a cross and memorial.

The story does not end there. As a religious man with no heir, he had written a will that stated that whichever church buried his body would get his lands in Plymstock. This will was almost certainly well known, but still there is an embellishment to the story that the will was found on a piece of paper found by his body, written in blood.

And so there was a race on between the monks of **Tavistock**, who were closer to the site, and **Plymstock** who thought their claim to be stronger. Monks from both abbeys set out to claim his mortal remains and take them back for burial. Plymstock realised they would not get there in time and so devised a plan where they would intercept the Tavistock monks after retrieving Childe's body. This was planned for a bridge that the Tavistock monks would surely have to cross. An ambush was set.

Word of this somehow got to the Tavistock monks who then changed plan and crossed the river in a different place, having made a temporary bridge. Their evasion worked so that Childe was interred at Tavistock Abbey and his lands claimed. The bridge which was made more permanent later, became known as "Guile Bridge" but its location is not clear.

Abbey ruins in Tavistock

Abbot's lodging remains - Betsy Grimbal's Tower

Kitty Jay's Grave near Hound Tor

Kitty Jay

Another sad tale that still survives today, perhaps quoted as a salutary lesson, is that of Kitty Jay. She was a young girl apprenticed to work at a farm near **Manaton**. A hard life with little respite or reward; she found herself receiving the attention of a local boy, probably the son of the farmer. It seems she was seduced by him and was destined to be an unmarried mother when her lover betrayed her and left her to be persecuted alone. This was clearly a fate worse than death. She hanged herself in one of the farm barns.

At that time, suicide was 'self-murder' and the body could not be buried on consecrated ground. Like so many other suicides of the time, she was interred at a crossroads at the parish boundary, so that her spirit would not return to haunt the village.

"Jay's Grave" can be seen at a crossroads about a mile north west of **Hound Tor**. Legend has it that there are always fresh flowers upon her grave; although no one has ever seen them being placed.

As an anecdote to Kitty Jay's story, around 1860 a local named James Bryant, who owned the nearby Hedge Barton, decided to see if there was truth to the tale. He had the grave excavated and indeed the skull and bones of a young woman was found. He then had her remains placed in a wooden box and re-interred in the same place, but had a burial mount raised around it to mark it more fittingly.

There are other grave sites for people who chose death over life. At a crossroads of paths near **White Tor**, there is Stephen's Grave, inscribed with an 'S', marking the resting place of a young man's whose love was unrequited.

Stephen's Grave, near White Tor

Hairy Hands Road

By far the most bizarre and unique story of Dartmoor; the 'Hairy Hands' haunt a section of the B3212 road between **Two Bridges** and **Postbridge**. No mention of this story exists before around 1920, but what the story lacks in age, it makes up for in absurdity.

So, let me take you back to around 1920. There was a series of accidents on this particular stretch of road that could not be explained. Pony traps had veered off, overturning into ditches, cyclists and motorcyclists had lost control and crashed. There was a Princetown doctor who was riding his motorbike with two children in the sidecar when the engine suddenly detached itself. The children were thrown clear but the doctor was killed. The strange sequence of accidents culminated with an army officer who was riding his motorbike when he crashed.

This army officer stated at the time that just before the crash, he was aware of a pair of large muscular hairy hands that closed over his own and forced the motorbike off the road. The story spread quickly and in 1921 the Daily Mail sent reporters to the area to investigate the truth of the story. "Hairy Hands on Dartmoor" was published and became an overnight sensation.

So much publicity led the local authorities to carry out their own investigation. The road was declared to be at fault - it had an adverse camber. Repairs were made and the problem fixed.

However, the stories of hairy hands and a malevolent spirit in the area continued. A few years later a woman described how she saw a hairy hand 'clawing' at the caravan window as her husband slept. As soon as she made the sign of the cross it disappeared.

Hairy Hands Road - B3212

Hairy Hands when you least expect them

Rationality would point out the fact that the road lies between two settlements both of which have hostelries that sell alcoholic beverages and that it may well be easier to blame a pair of supernatural dismembered metacarpi than admit to human error. How cynical that would be?

Later 'sightings' and tales posted online have refuelled the legend so that it remains a firm favourite of Dartmoor.

Sheepstor - site of Pixies House

Pixies and Fairies

Fairies have obviously long been the subject of tales, and have been attributed to mischievous meddling in the human world for as long as people have been perplexed by nature and/or partaking in a local draught of ale. The fairies are everywhere of course, not just in Devon, but it must be said that Dartmoor has more than its fair share.

There are place names all over the moor referencing the 'little folk", such as Pixies Holt near **Dartmeet** and Puggie Stone, **Chagford**; Puggie being interchangeable with Puck - the 'Arch Pixie', immortalised by William Shakespeare's Midsummer Night's Dream.

Entrance to Pixies House on Sheepstor

The best example is "Pixie's House" on the side of **Sheepstor**. The Ordnance Survey had the good grace to mark its presence on the current 1:25000 map; it must be real! Indeed there is a cave located there that is difficult to find and can hide several people at once. It is also a struggle to enter, being only big enough for pixies. Curious humans must plunge themselves head first into a dark hole at ground level, prising their bodies through strange angles to achieve a sitting position to view the trinkets deposited there.

Inside Pixie's House

Tangled traps of Wistman's Wood

Bowerman's Nose

Over on the east of Dartmoor there is a tall, strange rocky granite stack on **Hayne Down** near **Manaton** called "Bowerman's Nose". It looks somewhat like a human figure wearing a hat. This is what is left of Bowerman the Hunter, a giant of a man who settled on a nearby farm after the Norman conquest. Was he a bow-man perhaps? Legend has him riding the moor with his pack of hounds, hunting happily, chasing a hare when he came across a coven of witches who were angered by his disturbance. Bowerman, who was not afraid of them, laughed and carried on. The witches gained their revenge. One of them shape-shifted into a hare and lured him into an ambush. He was cast into stone. The locals liked Bowerman and so they overcame their fears and drove out the witches forever.

Wisht Hounds

Another hunter and another pack of hounds; this time sketchy folklore called them the Wisht Hounds, belonging to none other than the Devil himself, "Dewer" as he's known locally. His huge black demon hounds head out on wild stormy nights, hunting for both animals and humans, their cries carried in the wind. It is said that if you hear the cries of the Wisht Hounds you will die within a year.

Their favoured hunting ground is supposed to be **Wistman's Wood** near the ancient path called Lych Way - "Way of the Dead". The roots and boulders of Wistman's Wood slow down the hunted to their inevitable end. Another favoured spot is the **Dewerstone**, near Shaugh Prior, where Dewer would drive men over the crag for him to collect at the bottom. Charming.

Bowerman's Nose on Hayne Down near Manaton

Broad Rock boundary marker

White Moor boundary marker

"Mistorrpan" - 1609 Perambulation marker

Customs

Beating the Bounds

This really is an ancient custom, probably established around a thousand years ago but almost certainly dating back to the Bronze Age when marking and using territorial bounds reinforced tribal lands and village claims. Boundaries of earth and stone walls were built, known as reaves, with standing stones and other stone markers used for demarcation.

In medieval times boundary stones would have been erected to mark parish boundaries. Parishioners would walk around the boundary 'beating' the markers with a rod or wand of wood. Youngsters were brought along so that the markers' positions were passed on to later generations.

The custom had a revival during the 20th century in many parishes. If nothing else, it provides a grand day out on the moor.

The original Dartmoor boundary was that of Dartmoor Forest - the central portion of land granted to Richard, Earl of Cornwall in 1239 by his brother King Henry III. The Forest needed to be marked and defined; twelve knights were commissioned to travel the boundary and record its delineation in perpetuity. This was the 1240 Perambulation.

Another recorded Perambulation was undertaken in 1609, which clarified and modified some of the original 1240 marker points. This included "Mistorrpan" on **Great Mis Tor**, which defined the new marker point as the large rock basin situated on top of the tor. The Perambulation is over 40 miles long and has been perambulated many times since; a famous and well-loved long distance path on Dartmoor today.

Boundary stones near Higher Tor - Okehampton Parish (OP B) and Belstone Bound Parish (BB)

One of the Forest boundary markers can be found at **South Hessary Tor**, close to Princetown. On top of the tor there is a short vertical rod of iron with a flattened tip, rather like a cobra. On it are inscribed the letters of 'FB' (Forest Boundary) on one side and 'W' (Walkhampton parish) on the other. Originally there were 4 of these iron markers delineating the boundary between Walkhampton and the Forest. Now only two survive, at South Hessary Tor and the other at **Eylesbarrow**. The rods seen today are not original; they are replicas to replace the originals from 1867.

Dartmoor Forest Boundary Marker

Ponsworthy Splash and the old bridge

TOWNS & VILLAGES

Dartmoor's intrinsic charm does not finish where the fields end and the streets begin; the towns, villages and hamlets on Dartmoor deliver their own delight.

Scattered all over the moor, there are clusters of ancient buildings and thatched cottages that nestle within Dartmoor's lanes. Many of the towns can trace back their history to over a thousand years ago, and are linked inextricably with either the trade and travel routes of monks (at **Buckfast**, **Buckland** and **Tavistock Abbeys**), or they were key to the medieval tin mining industry. Dartmoor's smelted tin was assayed and coined at four Stannary Towns at **Tavistock**, **Plympton**, **Ashburton** and **Chagford**. Tavistock and Plympton are just outside the National Park boundary. **Lydford** was the administrative centre for the Royal Forest of Dartmoor and all Stannary Law and enforcement.

Dartmoor's towns are distinguished by their original granite buildings surrounded by newer buildings from later eras, when Dartmoor was 're-discovered' as a visitor attraction.

Widecombe-in-the-Moor

Widecombe is perhaps the most famous Dartmoor town; immortalised by the folk song "Widecombe Fair" featuring the characters of 'Old Uncle Tom Cobley and All'. It is very much a honeypot for visitors, with multiple car parks, cafés, pubs and gift shops. It is remarkable and a credit to itself that its popularity has not spoilt its ambience. The town is still a delight to visit; its historic buildings and welcoming businesses ensure that visitors return year after year.

Pepperport Market House in Chagford

The "Cathedral of the Moor" Church of St Pancras at Widecombe-in-the-Moor

Widecombe-in-the-Moor village centre

The focus of the village is the church and adjacent church house. Known as the 'Cathedral of the Moor', Widecombe's Church of St Pancras was originally built in the 14th century and subsequently enlarged with a particularly high 36m tower which dominates the East Webburn river valley in which it sits.

The church tower's original demise was due to a famous storm. On Sunday 21st October 1638, there was an intense thunderstorm overhead. Darkness overwhelmed the church so that it was hard to see, when suddenly lightning shot through the church, with a ball of fire. One of the tower's pinnacles was struck by the lightning and fell through the roof. In all, four people in the congregation were killed and sixty-two injured.

Next to it is the Church House, built around 1537 from large granite blocks. Like all old church houses, it was built to accommodate parish festivities and the brewing of ale for such occasions. Widecombe's Church House is one of the finest examples surviving in Britain.

Church House at Widecombe-in-the-Moor

The front of the Church House is a colonnade with seven granite pillars over granite cobbles. In the middle there is a large 15" naval shell on display. This is a memorial presented to Widecombe as a thank you to the people of the village who collected sphagnum moss from the moorland bogs which was then used as emergency field dressings for wounded service personnel in the First World War.

Naval shell at the Church House

Widecombe Fair

Dating back to the early 1800s when farmers would gather from surrounding farms and hamlets in the autumn to trade livestock, Widecombe Fair has since become so much more. It now takes place on the second Tuesday of September every year and attracts thousands of visitors from far and wide.

These days locals still show their livestock, but the fair also offers arts, crafts, music and family activities for all. There is a strong rural feel and acknowledgement of its agricultural roots, whilst raising money for local causes.

Of course, 'Old Uncle Tom Cobley' still rides around the village re-enacting the days of old, when he rode his 'old grey mare' to the fair.

The Green at Widecombe-in-the-Moor

Chagford

Endecott House at Chagford

Entrance to Three Crowns at Chagford

Chagford was a Saxon town called "Kagefort" meaning 'Gorse Ford', and is recorded in the Domesday Book of 1086. It sits near the River Teign on the north east of Dartmoor. Its prominence, however, arose from medieval tin mining. In 1305, King Edward I granted Chagford a Stannary Town Charter; one of four Stannary towns of Dartmoor.

Tinners would bring their ingots of smelted tin on pack-horses to the town where they would be assayed, weighed and 'coined'; the tin owner then having to pay the appropriate tax to the Crown. Wool was also important too; enough to have a wool factory between 1800 and 1845 making blankets and serge from local fleeces brought to market.

Chagford is steeped in history and it shows. The Church of St Michael was dedicated in 1261. The town buildings exude both history and charm. The Three Crowns Hotel, built in the 13th century, stoops opposite the church. In 1643, Sidney Godolphin (a Cavalier who was also a poet and MP) was shot and killed here during a Civil War skirmish and carried into the hotel's porch.

The market square at the centre of the town is instantly recognisable by the octagonal "Pepperpot" market house, built in 1862 on the site of a 16th century market and court house.

Chagford today is a compact and delightful market town; full of shops, businesses and hostelries. It has a reputation for arts, crafts and fine food. With a car park just outside of town, the accessibility of this moorland town is much improved. Chagford is clearly prosperous and a quintessential market town of Dartmoor.

15th century Bishops House in Chagford

Lydford

Just inside the western edge of Dartmoor National Park is Lydford, original called 'Hlidaford' in Saxon times when it was one of the 'Burhs' of Devon designated by Alfred the Great. Many Saxon features remain: the town layout is still a classic Saxon grid, and remnants remain of the 10th century earthworks that were constructed to defend against Cornish tribes and the Vikings. The Vikings tried to raid Lydford in 997AD, after sailing into Plymouth, but were repelled. They went on to destroy Tavistock Abbey. At the time, Lydford was hugely important and had its own mint producing silver pennies; the main currency throughout the Kingdom of Wessex.

Lydford Castle and Stannary Gaol

After the Norman Conquest in 1066 a new castle was built. Ramparts and ditches from this rare early Norman castle (the *original* Lydford Castle) can still be explored today in the field behind the church. It was abandoned fairly quickly and in 1195 King John authorised the building of a new tower nearby to become the administrative centre for the entire Royal Forest of Dartmoor and the Stannary Court of Devon. 'Lydford Law' was famously harsh; a person would be hanged first and tried later. This three-storey castle with its own dungeon still stands tall and imposing today.

These days Lydford is mainly residential, with a wonderful pub aptly named "The Castle" and a church that dates back to the 13th century.

Nearby is National Trust owned **Lydford Gorge**; a spectacular wooded ravine at the bottom of which the River Lyd carves out great cauldrons in the dark rock. Further along the gorge a 30 metre high 'White Lady Waterfall' drops water from the River Burn into the River Lyd below.

Lydford Gorge

Ashburton

Ashburton lies at the eastern edge of the National Park, near the A38. Its history goes back to before the Domesday Book when it was recorded as "Essebreton", but it was as one of the four Stannary Towns of Dartmoor that its prominence grew. It was designated a Stannary around 1285 where tin was assayed, weighed, coined and sold. Indeed it was the most important of the four Stannaries during medieval tin mining; by 1515 nearly 40% of Devon's tin was sold through Ashburton.

West Street, Ashburton

The town is a delight and gains its name from the River Ashburn that flows right through the middle of it; negotiating town buildings before flowing south west to meet the Dart.

A particular feature of the town's buildings is that many are faced with slate; some of which have special significance. The Card House is famous for having slates carved with the suits of cards - it was once a gaming house.

River Ashburn through Ashburton Town

Ashburton is also one of only eight towns in England that hold the ancient Saxon office of 'Portreeve'. Its literal meaning is market place official, and the incumbent was the Crown's representative who ensured taxes and trading were conducted properly. It is a position that dates back to 820AD and is still appointed today. Each year the Court Leet elects the Portreeve, together with his Bailiff, Ale Tasters, Bread Weighers and lesser offices.

Buckfast

Not far from Ashburton is Buckfast. This is where Buckfast Abbey was built as a monastery during the reign of King Cnut

East Street, Ashburton

Buckfast Abbey and Monastery

in 1018. The abbey has been an intrinsic part of Dartmoor ever since. Nearby is the small town of **Buckfastleigh,** which is thought to have developed as a supporting settlement to the abbey. The town grew prosperous from woollen mills and leather tanning. Situated at the confluence of the River Mardle and Dean Burn, it was well placed for using water to power many mills.

Buckfast Abbey was originally founded as a Benedictine order, but changed to the Cistercian Order in 1147. During medieval

Monastery buildings built from limestone

Moretonhampstead and Sparrowhawk

Sparrowhawk of Moretonhampstead

Court Street buildings, Moretonhampstead

times, the Cistercians became the country's main wool producers and exporters. In 1539, the abbey was surrendered to Dissolution and its wealth and treasures confiscated.

Over the years, the buildings changed ownership, became ruined and re-used until the site was taken on by a group of monks exiled from France in 1882. The monks started a project to rebuild the abbey. It took until 1937 for the final stone to be laid on the tower. More often than not, the building work was undertaken by just four monks.

Now, Buckfast Abbey is completely self-sufficient; farming cattle and pigs, as well as growing vegetables and herbs. It is a major tourist attraction and famous for its beekeeping; selling honey and beeswax as well as other goods in its gift shop. Its other famous export is Buckfast Tonic Wine.

Moretonhampstead

Since being granted a market charter in 1207 by King John, Moretonhampstead has been a bustling Dartmoor town. It is a gateway to eastern Dartmoor and offers a variety of shops, facilities and interesting buildings.

Its origins are Saxon and it was recorded in the Domesday Book of 1086 as 'Mortone'; meaning farmstead in moorland. The town grew steadily during the Middle Ages and prospered until the end of the 17th century when the wool industry declined. It has remained an important Dartmoor trading town and offers both history and modern amenity to visitors.

The sparrowhawk seen flying from a wall in the town centre is a modern sculpture by Roger Dean. When King John granted the

Almshouses in Moretonhampstead

town its charter, the rent was set at one sparrowhawk per year. It has become symbolic of the town.

One of the best buildings that has survived the ravages of time and fire is the Almshouses in Cross Street. Although the entrance shows the date as 1637, the solid granite building was actually constructed in 1451 as a hospital. It was refurbished into eight single room dwelling almshouses in 1637. During the 18th century it was known as the poorhouse, and in 1952 it was finally given to the National Trust.

Entrance to Almshouses in Moretonhampstead

Princetown, with the prison behind

Old Police Station building and green

Dartmoor Brewery at Princetown

Princetown

A new town on Dartmoor, by comparison! At 435m above sea level Princetown is the highest settlement on Dartmoor and was founded in 1785 by Sir Thomas Tyrwhitt who was Private Secretary to the then Prince of Wales. Tyrwhitt leased a large area of moorland with the intention of 'improving it' so that it was fit for profitable agriculture.

He also built Dartmoor Prison in 1806 for Napoleonic prisoners of war. "Prince's Town" was truly established as a functional settlement that served both agriculture and penal incarceration.

Much of Princetown's buildings reflect its late Georgian heyday; the best of which is the 1810 Duchy Hotel building in the centre. This is now the principal **Dartmoor National Park Visitor Centre**; an award-winning centre with interactive displays, exhibitions and information.

The Visitor Centre stocks a wide range of Dartmoor products and books as well as souvenirs and guide books. There is also the 'Conan Doyle Study' - recreating the time when he stayed at the Duchy Hotel and was inspired to write the *Hound of the Baskervilles*. The Centre's staff can give advice and suggestions for ways to explore the National Park safely.

Princetown is an adventure hub; where walkers, cyclists and expeditioners often congregate to start and end their adventures. The many cafés and pubs offer sustenance for all.

The Dartmoor Brewery started out as a micro-brewery in the back of the Prince of Wales pub in 1994, where it brewed the first batch of its now famous 'Jail Ale'. It is now one of Devon's largest breweries.

Dartmoor National Park Visitor Centre in the old Duchy Hotel in Princetown

Historic wild landscapes exist alongside modern on Dartmoor

DARTMOOR TODAY

Dartmoor is an ancient landscape, but it is also one that has to fit with contemporary living. The challenge of preserving the past whilst preparing for the future is not without difficulty or compromise. Business, farming, industry, tourism and recreation must somehow bump along together; united by legacy and the desire to make the best of Dartmoor. This is one of Dartmoor's triumphs; industry and important habitats exist side-by-side; farmers have diversified to incorporate tourism, conservation and recreation into their business.

A living place that ignores the need for change and stands still like a museum is destined for death. Gladly, Dartmoor is thriving; new ventures that make the most of Dartmoor's unique character freshen the economy and increase the overall appeal that Dartmoor has for visitors. Dartmoor National Park Authority is the framework that maintains the balance.

Industry

China Clay
China clay is essentially decomposed granite. Whilst the mica and quartz crystals of the granite remained unaffected by underground chemical weathering and geologic hydrothermal activity, the feldspar crystals were not. In areas where the feldspars had more sodium than potassium, the feldspar crystals were broken down into a white inert powdery material called 'kaolin'.

Kaolin was named after a mountain village in China called "Kao-ling", which was the first to mine the material for making porcelain some 1700 years ago; hence its adopted name.

East Dart River near Bellever

China Clay Works at Lee Moor

Kaolin extraction

With the increasing need of 19th century potteries (they did like their china), local sources were investigated, found and quickly exploited. Kaolin was extracted by using water to move the loose material into a series of settling pits where the heavier quartz and mica were separated out, eventually settling on the bottom. Eventually the water would only contain the kaolin in suspension. This was then left to stand in pools before being drained and dried. In 2000, dry mining was introduced whereby dry rock material was removed to a separate wet processing plant to be extracted.

Although other sites have been mined for kaolin, it is **Lee Moor** that remains the most extensive area of china clay workings on Dartmoor. It has grown over the years and remains a hugely important contributor to Dartmoor's economy as well as its changing landscape.

Kaolin is inert and is used to produce not only porcelain, but paper, sanitary wear, medicines, tennis balls and white lines on roads. 80% of the area's china clay is exported around the world. The industry is a significant contributor to UK trade.

Mining

Much of Dartmoor's landscape has been shaped by historical mining; for tin, copper and arsenic. The scars of the industrial landscape have healed over and now offer both recreational and archaeological interest.

Tin mining on Dartmoor had more or less stopped by the First World War due to other global sources and changing economies. Tungsten, however, was a different matter. Also known as Wolfram, tungsten is a highly valuable hardening agent in steel manufacture and due to its extraordinarily high melting point, has been used in light bulbs, casings for drill bits as well as military applications.

On the southern tip of Dartmoor at **Hemerdon Ball**, there is a tungsten mine. In the First World War, mining for this highly sought after mineral was open cast, but during the 1940s shafts were cut into the ground. Operations ceased in 1944.

In 2015, Wolf Minerals Limited reopened the mine and expanded it. The Hemerdon tungsten deposit is vast and the mine is one of only two outside of China with production

Kaolin pit near Trowlesworthy Tors

Hemerdon Ball Tungsten Mine

Herding sheep on the high moor

Moving cattle to new fields

Farmland below Cox Tor

capacity greater than 3,000 tonnes per annum tungsten concentrate. The mine also produces tin, but on a lesser scale. Clearly, Dartmoor's mineral wealth and legacy is not confined to history just yet.

Farming

Farming anywhere is dictated by the climate and soil. With very high levels of rain, low temperatures, exposure to wind and poor soils, Dartmoor is very much a marginal farming area. It takes a great deal of effort to make even a small profit. Only livestock agriculture offers viable farming: sheep and cattle forming the bulk of Dartmoor farmers' herds.

Historically, Dartmoor farmers graze cattle, sheep and ponies on their enclosed pastures as well as on the open moor. They have the legacy of 'Dartmoor Commoner's' rights, allowing them to use the open moor for grazing. Some of these rights date back to the 13th century.

High moorland farms are characterised by poor, thin soils in larger newtake areas divided by stone walls. Lower altitude farms and those on the edges of the moor tend to be more productive with better soils and good pasture divided by traditional hedges.

Due to the growing season for grass being so much shorter on Dartmoor, there is less food for livestock to eat - grass, hay and silage - which means farmers have to move their cattle off the higher moor or buy in extra food over winter.

Dartmoor's farmers and livestock are hardy breeds. They have to be to survive the climate as well as the pressures of earning

Farmland surrounding Bellever Tor

a living in an increasingly difficult time for agriculture and acting as caretakers for a national recreation area.

Farm Animals

Dartmoor's sheep population is over 100,000. They all belong to different farmers and are marked as such. Unlike other livestock on the moor, the sheep are trained to stay in the area to which they were originally introduced, known as 'learing' on Dartmoor. This is essential for farmers to locate their flocks. In autumn, lambs are sold for fattening on lower pastures.

Scotch Blackface Sheep

Farming on Dartmoor today

Managing grazing on Dartmoor requires skill and experience to maintain both good pasture as well as biodiversity. 'Conservation Grazing' plays a hugely important role in keeping Dartmoor alive and well.

Dartmoor Scotch Blackface Sheep Shelter against the winter winds

Belted Galloway Cattle

The most common sheep to be found on Dartmoor is the Dartmoor Scotch Blackface. However, older breeds can be seen; including the Whiteface Dartmoor and Greyface Dartmoor sheep, known for their long curly fleeces.

When exploring Dartmoor, you are most likely to see Galloway cattle; both brown and black. Often they are Belted Galloways with the distinctive white band around their bellies, like corsets. Also seen are Aberdeen Angus and Devon Reds. Perhaps the most glorious are the occasional herd of Highland Cattle you might come across; long shaggy coats and fabulous horns, they take the prize for looking at home on the open moor.

Military

The subject of military training on Dartmoor has always been hotly debated. The Armed Forces have trained here since the early 1800s; using Dartmoor's unique landscape to develop a wide range of military and fieldcraft skills.

The Ministry of Defence owns or leases nearly 33,000 acres of the National Park including half of its high moorland. There are three defined Danger Areas where live firing is carried out on scheduled days; **Okehampton**, **Willsworthy** and **Merrivale**. These areas are surrounded by red flags by day and red lights by night to indicate when they are in use. During such times, public access is denied. There is also a 'dry' training area around Sheepstor, Ringmoor and Cramber, where military training is carried out without the use of live ammunition.

There is no doubt that live firing on Dartmoor has changed the landscape of Dartmoor; particularly on the north moor where artillery firing used to be carried out. However, the legacy of military landscape with its remnant target railways and trenches now form part of the appeal to a Dartmoor visitor.

One can argue that the Military's Dartmoor legacy is as valid as our Victorian forebears. In terms of the value of Dartmoor as a training ground, there is much evidence to support its huge benefit to training the Armed forces. A significant example is the success of the British Military personnel who retook the Falklands in 1982 having trained on Dartmoor where the climate and ground were so similar and challenging.

Highland cattle near Hameldown

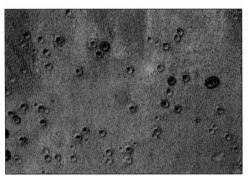
Steel butt at firing range near Rowtor

Range warning red flag at Roos Tor

Ten Tors

In 1960 the British Army held the very first Ten Tors Expedition. Since then, it has grown to become a monumental event in thousands of teenagers' lives. Every May, some 2400 teenagers set out from **Okehampton Army Camp** on different routes covering one of three distances; 35, 45 or 55 miles. They carry everything they need to camp out in the wilderness.

Hiking on Dartmoor is not like any other long distance path route. The ground is extremely difficult and lacks both signposts and paths as a rule. The teenagers have to learn navigational and fieldcraft skills as well as resilience and teamwork.

The British Army organises and runs this highly sought after expedition together with the Royal Navy, RAF, Dartmoor Rescue Group and many other agencies. Getting a place on a Ten Tors team is an achievement in itself. Completing it is something else that is never forgotten.

Tourism

Dartmoor is 368 square miles of rural landscape and wilderness; with 181 square miles of open moorland. It is beautiful, unusual and evokes a need to explore its treasures. It is no wonder that over 2.4 million people visit Dartmoor each year. The numbers keep increasing too as accessibility improves as well as awareness. Tourism is vital to the region's economy and Dartmoor represents a key destination to any visitor in the area.

There are two main roads that criss-cross the moor, offering access east to west, meeting at **Two Bridges**. Since the roads

Teams approaching Ten Tors checkpoint

Teams near finish of Ten Tors expedition

B3357 towards Two Bridges

were built, people have come to see the tors, rivers, woods and animals. There is truly something for everyone; whether it is sitting by a stream listening to the water babble down hidden cascades, watching cotton grass wiggle in the wind, or striding out to Fur Tor for backpack camping in the high moorland.

Clearly, the more people there are using certain areas of the National Park, the more erosion there is and its attraction compromised. The **Dartmoor National Park Authority** has a duty to conserve and enhance the quality of the landscape, as well as promoting its enjoyment and use. It is not an easy task as one can be detrimental to the other.

A balance is maintained through knowledge and education. Tourists now have so much more information about their destination than ever before; award winning visitor centres, information packs and online resources enable people to understand the consequences of their overall 'footprint' on Dartmoor.

So, what is it that attracts people to Dartmoor? Well, the moor can be all things to all people; but visitors usually have a few attributes that consistently top the list.

Bronze Age Beardown Man near Devil's Tor

Dartmoor Tors

The tors are the crags of rock that emerge from the hills creating a truly unique landscape. Most of them are granite; but there are some that are not, situated around the edge of the upland massif. Tors are the remnants of much larger outcrops of solid rock that have been shattered and scattered by freeze-thaw action during the Ice Ages. The broken fragments from the tors are the rocks and boulders that litter the hillsides and are collectively called 'clitter'.

Black Tor, on the West Okement Valley

Leather Tor overlooking Burrator Reservoir

Combestone Tor, overlooking the Dart Valley Nature Reserve

Fur Tor - the most remote of Dartmoor's tors

There are about 350 rocky outcrops on Dartmoor, but not all are called 'tors'; in fact there are only 154 named tors within the National Park, as marked on the Ordnance Survey 1:25,000 map of Dartmoor and on publicly accessible land. *Dartmoor Tors Compendium* describes them all, together with all the features surrounding each one.

A typical granite tor looks like it has been built from giant rounded blocks and giant hands; battered by the elements. Some are so remote that only dedicated walkers have seen them; like **Fur Tor** which lies in the middle of the north moor about 5km from the nearest vehicle track, as the crow flies.

Many other beautiful tors are, however, close to roads. **Combestone Tor** is especially worthy of a visit and is only 40m from the road between **Hexworthy** and **Holne**. It has many stacks, fabulous views over the **Dart Valley** and excellent examples of rock basins on the top of the granite outcrops.

Another easily accessible tor, with oodles of history is **Crockern Tor**. This important tor sits more or less in the very middle of Dartmoor, near the B3212 between **Two Bridges** and **Postbridge**. It is the site of the medieval Stannary Parliament; here the laws governing the mining and coining of Dartmoor's tin were made and enforced, from the early 1300s. Around 100 men (known as 'stannators') from all four tin mining Stannary towns (Tavistock, Chagford, Ashburton and Plympton) would gather around 'Parliament Rock' for open air governance. The last recorded meeting of the Stannary Parliament was in 1703.

Parliament Rock has steps leading to a natural platform and the tor clitter has many benches and tables fashioned from assembling slabs of granite. Sir Walter Raleigh was Lord Warden of the Stannaries in the early 1600s.

Dartmoor Ponies

Synonymous with Dartmoor is the fabled Dartmoor pony. Ponies have roamed Dartmoor's landscape since the Bronze Age. They are not wild as such; all are owned by different farmers who round them up each year in the autumn 'drift'. However, they are untamed and can be unpredictable. Once assembled, the farmers choose which ponies should stay on the moor and which are sold.

Parliament Rock at Crockern Tor

Rock table at Crockern Tor

A mare and her foal on Dartmoor

Hill ponies at Ger Tor above Tavy Cleave

Hill ponies on western edge of Dartmoor

The ponies play a vital role; their grazing helps maintain different habitats and biodiversity.

The true Dartmoor Pony is a breed registered with the Pony Club and kept in pony studs and no longer seen on the open moor. Most of the hill ponies seen on Dartmoor have a mixed gene pool. In addition to single coloured ponies that share the same ancestors as the pedigree Dartmoor Pony, there are hill ponies have been bred for their mixed colouring. Small ponies are the result of breeding with Shetlands which were used in mines. What unites them all is their hardiness, calm nature and strength. These ponies stay out in all weathers and actually thrive despite the poor weather and vegetation.

Whenever you see the ponies roaming on Dartmoor, and frequently crossing roads, be sure to slow down for them; remember they are untamed and never feed them.

Sherlock Holmes

Staying in Princetown's Duchy Hotel, now the **Dartmoor National Park Visitor Centre**, Sir Arthur Conan Doyle was inspired to write the *Hound of the Baskervilles in 1901*. It is fair to say that his literary creation has had a big impact on Dartmoor. Think of his eponymous detective Sherlock Holmes and it conjures up visions of dark, fog-bound nights when the merciless wind carries the howl of hounds and screams of those lost in Grimpen Mire.

Holmes aficionados agree that the inspiration for Grimpen Mire was **Fox Tor Mire**; truly a forbidding and dangerous place for those who do not know where to cross it. Merripit House was probably inspired by **Nun's Cross Farm** and the abandoned tin mine near the mire was almost certainly **Whiteworks** ruins. All these locations are close together just south of Princetown from the road to Peat Cot.

Fox Tor Mire is dangerous and most walkers should avoid it if possible. It is a quaking mass of water, peat and plant life that knows no solidity for its roots.

That is not to say there is not a path across; there is, but not where it is marked on the Ordnance Survey map, strangely. Local knowledge is essential in traversing the mire.

Sherlock Holmes at Princetown Visitor Centre

Nun's Cross Farm near Princetown

Whiteworks and Fox Tor Mire near Princetown

Trail running on Dartmoor

Exploring Dartmoor on foot

Road cycling across Dartmoor

Recreation

There is walking, riding, trail running, rock climbing, kayaking, wild swimming, backpack camping, mountain biking, letterboxing, geocaching as well as just 'being'. Sometimes, Dartmoor fulfils a need by just being there; smelling the peaty earth and listening to a skylark.

Walking

Dartmoor is a paradise for walkers of all ages, abilities and preferences. There are marked easy trails as well as a horizon full of remote wilderness where paths and signposts are notably absent. Then there is everything in between!

Ask at any Visitor Centre and you will receive masses of information about short walks, routes and places to see. There are leaflets and countless guide books which will open up the moors for you at your own pace. For the more adventurous, there are again many guide books written specifically for walks of a few hours to a whole day. For those who yearn for distance, wilderness and solitude; there is a map and compass. If you head out into the moor, make sure you know how to navigate. Always take the right equipment and always let someone know where you are going.

Cycling

Ever since the Tour of Britain first visited Dartmoor, the area has attracted many cyclists who love the challenge of the hills combined with stunning views.

Off-road cycling on mountain bikes is rapidly gaining in popularity. There is a map especially for mountain bikers which shows all the routes available. It must be stressed that cycling off-road is only permitted on bridle paths and permitted routes, of which there are plenty - around 350km. One of the most rewarding cycling routes on the moor is the *'Granite and Gears'* **Princetown** to **Burrator** route which follows the line of the disused railway through spectacular scenery and is mostly all downhill!

Off-road cycling route on disused railway

Horse Riding

The open moor provides an outstanding backdrop to horse riding, which offers people a unique perspective of Dartmoor. There are several riding stables around and on the moor where you can explore the open land and all the bridleways.

Rock Climbing

The tors and crags of Dartmoor offer climbers a full range of routes, with both superb scenery and easy access over open moorland. Climbing has been popular here for decades, but bouldering has transformed Dartmoor's shorter crags into perfect technical bouldering locations. That is not to say there is a lack of long routes. The **Dewerstone** has some excellent multi-pitch routes and **Haytor Rocks** provides perhaps the most exposed set of long granite faces to climb.

Enjoying the freedom of horse riding on Dartmoor

Kayaking

The rivers around Dartmoor are some of the best in the country for white water fun in a kayak. However, kayaking on Dartmoor's inland rivers is not generally permitted except on the River Dart below **Dartmeet**, during the winter between 1st October and 31st March each year. This helps protect the Dart Valley which is designated as a Special Area of Conservation

Climbing at Sheepstor

Kayaking on the Dart

Old letterbox at Rippon Tor

Inside a letterbox

and Site of Special Scientific Interest. There are access points at Dartmeet, Newbridge, Holne Weir and the Dartbridge cafe.

Kayaking on the Dart, especially when in spate, can be extremely dangerous for inexperienced paddlers. Please follow safety advice from the British Canoeing website.

Letterboxing and Geocaching

If only James Perrott of Chagford knew what he was starting in 1854 when he put out the very first letterbox at **Cranmere Pool** on Dartmoor! Visitors would leave their cards in the jar; later they would leave postcards which would then be picked up by the next person and posted. Later, letterboxes were placed at **Taw Marsh** (1894), **Ducks Pool** (1938), **Fur Tor** (1951) and **Crow Tor** (1962). Since then it has grown exponentially. It is quite possible to meet a letterboxer at a remote spot on Dartmoor who has collected tens of thousands of letterbox stamps - the ink imprint of the rubber stamps found in each box.

The letterboxes are found using clues; distances from features, grid references, bearings and paces. It is basically a treasure hunt. Boxes are usually tupperware containers holding a notebook, pen and rubber stamp, and are maintained by individuals. They are not permanent fixtures and so over the years, a letterboxer can build up an impressive collection. The informal *Letterbox 100 Club* publishes catalogues of clues to its members. Competence with a map, compass and pacing is honed from the beginning with this hobby!

From its beginning at Cranmere Pool, letterboxing gave rise to geocaching. As soon as Global Positioning System (GPS) devices became available to walkers, positions of boxes could be even more hidden and challenging. Geocaches can be tiny and disguised as almost anything. A keen eye and an ability to locate a cache with a 10 figure grid reference is required to be part of this global phenomenon. For more details, see *www. geocaching.com* for more details.

Backpack Camping

Camping on Dartmoor can be an exhilarating and fulfilling experience, when done properly. Large and family tents are only permitted on designated camp sites.

Backpack camping on Dartmoor

The only permitted camping allowed on Dartmoor is backpack camping, as part of a walking expedition. You are allowed to pitch a small tent for one or two nights in some areas of open moorland, well away from roads and settlements. Campers must travel light, stay out of sight, blend into the landscape and leave no trace. That means not lighting fires, and taking home rubbish and waste. There is an interactive camping map that shows where backpack camping is allowed on the Dartmoor National Park website.

Sunset over Dartmoor

Sometimes it is only when you camp in the wild, away from everyday life, that you see the most amazing light and scenery.

Sunrise over north Dartmoor

Looking east over the mist to Dartmoor

INFORMATION

DARTMOOR NATIONAL PARK AUTHORITY

Parke
Bovey Tracey
Newton Abbot
Devon TQ13 9JQ
01626 832093
www.dartmoor.gov.uk

Dartmoor National Park Visitor Centres

Princetown:
Tavistock Road
Princetown
Yelverton
Devon PL20 6QF
01822 890414

Haytor:
Lower car park on B3387,
3 miles west of Bovey Tracey.
TQ13 9XT
01364 661520

Postbridge:
Main car park on B3212
Moretonhampstead to Two Bridges road
PL20 6TH
01822 880272

OTHER BODIES

Devon Wildlife Trust
Cricklepit Mill
Commercial Road
Exeter, Devon
EX2 4AB
www.devonwildlifetrust.org

National Trust
South West Regional Office - Killerton
Killerton House
Broadclyst
Exeter EX5 3LE
01392 881691
www.nationaltrust.org.uk/days-out/regionsouthwest/
devon

Dartmoor Military Firing Times
www.gov.uk/government/publications/dartmoor-
firing-programme

INDEX